T0284123

The Day I Left

Michelle Yu

Written with love in Rishikesh, India

December 2023

The Day I Left

© 2024, Michelle Yu

ISBN: 979-8-35094-653-6

For the Divine Mother

PART 1

PART 2

PART 3

Part 1

You cannot heal what you are
unwilling to bring into your awareness.

You cannot know light unless you know darkness.

The only way through is through.

1 – The day I left

I remember my heart beating out of my chest
As I lugged my suitcase down the stairs
My dog confused and anxious
"What if he catches me"
"Are the cameras watching"
I am scared

I remember the thoughts running through my head
"Where should I go"
"Is this the right move and decision"
My heart beating out of my chest
Luggage in the car
Backup phone numbers on a sticky note
Lock the door just incase

I remember the swollen eyes
Crying on the beach
My last memory with my dog
Before I dropped him back
I will never have another night in that house
I became a refugee in my home

The day I left

I remember the hotel
2 days of pure confusion

Walking around in a haze
Making plans and arrangements
Putting on an armor of courage
All the unknown ahead

I remember showing up at my parents' house
A moment of pause
Before going in
Bursting into tears on the driveway
Getting caught in the act
A worried look of concern
My dad's hug to console me

I remember the pure raw emotion
Entering my family home
Pride and ego pushed aside
Trying to explain what happened
Between sobs and tears
Years of compressed silence and secrecy
Bursting out the seams
Years of a projected image of perfection
Shattered to pieces

The day I left

I remember the relief
Of not having to hold it in anymore
My family's support
A good night's rest in my bed

My nervous system slowly beginning to relax

Relief, but they will never fully know
No one will ever fully understand
Nor will I have to explain myself
Why I left

I remember the video call
Our coach as a mediator
As I delivered my request to dissolve our marriage
The hardest conversation of my life
The hardest decision of my life

Swirls of emotions all around
Informing family and friends
One step at a time
One day at a time
One hour at a time
One minute at a time

Shame slowly fading
Distance allows for seeing things as they are
No more making excuses
No more denial

The day I left
... was the day I took my power back and became a
sovereign being again

The fog clouds lifted and the gaslighting dissipated
No longer a victim to manipulation

The day I left
... was the day I broke free from my own limitations
The day I stopped living for others
I consciously choose me
This is my life and this is what's best for me

The day I left
... was my liberation
The day I woke up and decided to consciously break all
the intergenerational cycles
Rewrite everything that isn't working

This stops with me.

The day I left...
was the greatest gift, for both of us
A deep act of pure love
The only way for us to evolve even higher
Highest need of the hour
My dharma

The day I left
... was a new beginning
The day I embarked on a new journey
To finally start living for me

2 – What happened

It's hard to pinpoint an exact moment
Of when a relationship falls apart
9 years vanished seemingly overnight
If only it was easy to explain

But they want to know
There is a curiosity
To pinpoint an answer
With a picture-perfect outside

What happened?

Maybe they want to know
Because of their own projected fears
That it might happen to them
Perhaps there's a piece of me
They see within themselves
Which might manifest their own reality

Or maybe it's from their own curiosity
Of what life is like on the other side
To take that leap of faith
Into the unknown
Fly solo
Will it be worth it

They want to know
Or maybe they don't want to know

What happened?

For some it happens slowly, slowly
Small daily interactions
Depleting the love bank
An emotional jab here and there
Overly sharp words hidden as a joke
A body gesture that evokes dominance

When it's the subtlest
It's not easy to see it for what it is
Lovers slowly dissolving into strangers

For others it happens hard and fast
Perhaps even blindsiding and shocking
An overly hard grasp that crossed boundaries
A bruise that left the faintest mark
Or maybe a blow to the face
A crude awakening
But is it ever really out of the blue?

They want to know
What happened

No one will ever fully understand
Nor do I need to share

In the end, everyone has their own interpretation

No one will ever walk a mile in my shoes
So I'll leave it to your imagination
To read between the lines
My story is just a story
With no attachment to be heard

Yet, they still want a pinpointed answer
The cliff notes version
A history of 9 years
Compressed into 500 words
Into a mere 3 minutes

So let's keep it simple:

Self-validation
Self-respect
Self-realization
Deep personal growth

What happened was that I found myself again
It took all my willpower to leave
And not look back
It took constant reminders
To not slip back into the "comfortable" shackles
It took a fuck ton of help and support
To stop gaslighting myself

Courage to walk through the fire
Strength and determination
Through dark times
Which in the end
Came light

What happened was I finally woke up and remembered
who I am
Strong and brave
I can choose a new path
From victim to victor
Whatever story I choose to write
A fresh start
I am not alone

What happened was I finally learned
The true meaning of self-love and self-trust
Above all
To value myself and my happiness
Standards high, but all within reason
I am not "too much"
I am worthy
I am free

In sharing comes awareness
In speaking comes healing

So now you know
What happened

3 – I'll say the things

I'll laugh when things are unnecessarily serious
Giggle during an off tune "OM" in yoga class
Be the first to openly admit my humanly indulgences
Instead of meditating this morning
I danced to "ratchet party slaps"
I want a hamburger

I'll say the things that are on your mind
You were thinking it
But I said it

I'll be the first to say
That our teacher is good looking
That breathing gets me high
And yoga makes me horny
It's really not that deep
Namaste

You were thinking it
But I said it

I'll say the things of what's on my heart
Whether it uplifting and funny
Or hard to swallow
I call it out if needed
From a place of love

I speak my truth

So naturally I was the first to say
That I wanted more
For us to go deeper
Though something always felt off
We were on different wavelengths

I feel alone

And after much passing time
Of continuous patterns
No growth or change
I finally said the thing
"This isn't working anymore"
When we both already knew
Deep down inside

The truth

You were thinking it
But I said it

Because someone had to address it
Take that first step
For a new beginning

When you don't say the thing

A muzzle to your mouth
An internal thrashing around
Dissonance
Lack of release
A part of you dies inside

Repression over the years
Is toxicity in the body

It's me that will say the things
When it seems too hard
Address what's been building for a while
So it can be released
Because somebody had to

So say the thing
No one can read your mind
Have the courage
Open the conversation
Don't sweep it under the rug

Because someone's probably thinking it already
You're just the one to say it

Your liberation awaits
On the other side of thought
Transmuted into words

4 – The body knows

The body remembers
The things we forget
Its innate wisdom is infinite

It especially remembers
Being told it doesn't work right
When made to feel like damaged goods

However modern medicine
Seems to provide solutions
Quick fixes and instant gratification
Hopes for a way forward

We wanted the short cut
A roadmap
As if running on autopilot
There was no pause

It all happened so fast

Ice pack
Alcohol swab
Hold the belly
Breathe
Small poke
Band-Aid
Next

Head to the clinic
Find the vein
Ultrasound
Monitor
Anesthesia
Next

Another day
Another needle
Hormones flood the system

I am bloated

Again
and again
and again
Until the red needle carton is full
Hoping it works out
What is actually happening?

Blurred vision
100 miles an hour

Where is the reflection?

Playing god the creator with the medicine
Roll the dice
Will this work?
More importantly

Will this fix my relationship?

Slow. down.

What is actually happening here?

Another day
Another needle
Groggy in recovery
A successful surgery

I am numb

Are you really ready for that next step?

Even if I didn't want kids
It would be cool to know that I could

Breathe.
Process.
Get clear.
Slow. down.

The body is not a checklist of to-dos
It remembers being treated as a piece of meat
Seen as a mere baby making vehicle
In hopes to create a family

A family that would save a relationship?

17

Everything feels so difficult
Is it supposed to be this fucking hard?

I feel alone

Breathe.
Process.
Be honest.
Slow. down.

We forget the body is intelligent
And it knew all along

When the mind wanted to fight
And the heart was in denial

The body intervened
Knowing
It wasn't meant to play out this way
My body was my wakeup call

Breathe.

Process.

Tune in.

Slow. down.

My body did for me
What my mind couldn't comprehend
Intentionally blocking the way forward
Until I could catch up
To see what was actually happening

Looking back
My body was hijacked
Internal pressure and a desire to control
Influenced by societal pressures
Familial conditioning

A puppet
Afraid to let go
Instead trying to yield my way
Into making things happen
Doing more damage than good

Breathe.

Process.

Heal.

Slow. Down.

As much as the body remembers
The pain it underwent

For discarded embryos
Stored on ice
It also remembers
The deep relief
From finally having clarity

Once the decision was made
Released into the world
Control surrendered
Good sleep
Repair my overworked nervous system
A returning bright smile

Breathe.

Release.

Heal.

Slow. Down.

With so much gratitude
I thank my body for the endless lessons
For slowing me down
And doing what my mind was in denial of

I am thankful

Dissecting everything months later
I vow to honor my body's innate wisdom
To treat it as a beautiful vessel
No longer through drive, force or control

Instead to allow for whatever should happen
To unfold and flow effortlessly
As nature intended

Breathe.

Purify.

Remember.

Slow. Down.

5 – My scars tell a story

Faint, but still there
Incisions cut deeper than they show

Healing, but who knows
What is happening under the surface

Fading, but still recovering
It's hard to forget the emotional impact

Commonly dismissed
Infrequently diagnosed

It took 7 years to figure out
What was happening in my body

Visit after visit
Routine ultrasound check ups
Only confirmed once under the knife

But it's just 3 small incisions
A surgery less than 2 hours
Plus it's so common amongst women

"You aren't anything special"
So stop making a big deal out of it
Shut your mouth
Stop talking about it

My scars tell a story
That anyone with endometriosis understands
The suffering in silence and confusion

Writing off symptoms
Dismissing the experience
It's just part of being a woman
Stop being dramatic and difficult

What no one shares
Perhaps the most painful scar of all
Is sitting with the reality and possibility
Of barrenness
A woman's natural birthright
My heart and ovaries ache

My scars tell a story
Because it screams
"Finally, you're paying attention"
"Thank you for doing something about it"

7 years of no answers
Made everything worse
Stagnant inflammation
Turns into infertility

Societal pressure and conditioning
To become a mother
A woman's expected path
Rarely a pause for deep consideration

My scars tell a story
Bringing light to who I could actually lean on
Who was listening
Who had my back during times of need
Are you on my side, or not?
Or am I just making a fuss
You just don't understand

No more rigidity and forcing my hand
With needles and medicine
I choose not to endure that process again
Instead honor my body's natural decline
Graceful geriatrics

My scars tell a story because it showed me
I had to change
The lifestyle and diet
My mindset
The doctor
And
My partner

Learning to fully accept
Surrender to the unknown
A home with maybe just fur-babies
Something a future partner
Should know and embrace

Scars heal over time
People in your life will come and go
In the end it all becomes just a memory
A blip in time that passes on
The emotional charge fades away

Peace

So here's my ode to that distant memory
A vow to leave behind
Resentment and bitterness
Against those 7 years of waiting
The doctor
Against those hurtful words used
My partner

Forgiveness

Like a woman's cycle
Shedding the old
Preparing a fresh foundation
A new moon
My scars, like my body
Will dissolve into nothingness

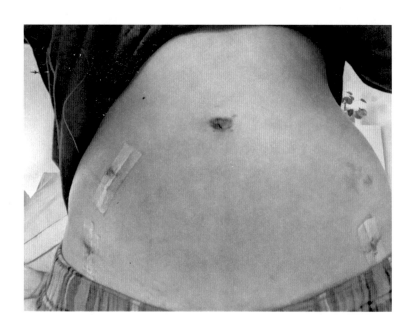

6 – Don't tell grandma

Don't tell grandma
The real reason behind why I left for India
She doesn't know about the year I've had
The needles and the scars
I don't want her to worry

We told her he won't be around anymore
That alone was plenty to take in
All the rest, she doesn't need to know
She's 96 and wise beyond years
She doesn't need the full story

Grandma helped raise me
I came from her womb
Three generations of women
I can't bear tell her the truth
There may not be a forth

My grandma is not old fashioned
She said so herself
Fairly understanding
But the truth simply hurts

Her little body can't take it
She's been through too much
When she fled for Hong Kong
That was already a lot

With her is not the right place to unpack
Such heaviness and shame
Plus with the language barrier
Makes it harder to share

So I put on a brave face
A smile through the eyes
Though it's not pretend
What I'd rather grandma see
Is my inner strength

I mirror her resilience
In a different way
Cutting through pressure, guilt and shame
From our own generation
We both work to close the loop

Pain turned to power
To face the unknown
I took my chances
Doing what women in our family couldn't do

I'll be the one to put a stop
Break the generational patterns
I prioritize healing and happiness
It's not easy work

It's okay though
Someone had to do it

To start the conversation
So generations learn and don't go through it

Liberate ourselves from the story
We're no longer in shackles
Create a new narrative
Let's set ourselves free

So I put on a happy face
Though it's not pretend
This is my karma
Part of my dharma

Don't tell grandma
One of our common phrases
Out of sheer love
It's better not to know

There's no need to feel sad
This moment is fleeting
Life simply continues
We will eventually move on

7 – Sattva

I found a place
To heal my wounds
A cocoon for my transformation

Who could ask for a better place
To process a divorce
And heal after an intense year of heartache

I flew around the world
In search for peace
Hiring help from all around

Dappled with the plants
Seeking wisdom
Pay my respects to Gaia

But I could not keep running
No one could take me deeper
I can't outsource my healing

The best healer is me

A tuning fork
To go deeply inward
Unveil a new consciousness

It wasn't my intention
I just wanted to learn yoga
Then something profound happened

Cry
Purge
Purify

I found my people
Transcended what happened
Freed myself from the shackles

Release it to the fire
Cleanse yourself in the river
Gaze into my eyes

With so much stillness
Calm and tranquility
You're bound to finally see clearly

When the dust settles
What channels through
Who are you?

Turns out she was there all along
Just waiting to be rediscovered
Liberated again

————————————————

At Sattva
I experienced sattva
A transcended me

A place to let it all go
Turn your mess into your message
Transform from victim to victor

A place to plant new seeds
Fine tune your vibration
Metamorphosis

In the end all that remains
Is the here and now
How will I share my story?

When I return home, what will be next?
I haven't thought that far
For I live in this moment, the here and now

Part 2

"Any practice is ultimately only
as good as the practitioner."

Anand Mehrotra

8 – Peaceful warrior

Now that you know
All I've expressed
Cat's out the bag
Take it slow and digest

Don't feel sad for me
It's not what I want
What I'd rather be remembered for
Is my inner strength

Because when you feel sad
I need to explain
That I'm working really hard
To rewire my brain

To let go of old conditioning
And see things a new
That I am not a victim
Instead I am free

Yes I've been through a lot
Probably more than you'll understand
Yet it's not without purpose
I have a strong stance

You see, the world is our oyster
Perception we can choose

To transcend and ascend
Are part of my great plans

Instead I have new aspirations
To be a bright flame
Burning with intention and precision
Steady with control

No wild bursts, no need for drama
Instead a clean, clear aura
Trauma transcended into gratitude
A yogi that doesn't project

Giving myself permission to be happy
I am my own self
Despite how they think I should behave
I chart my own path

If you still don't get it, that's okay
The hero's journey one must choose
With every circumstance comes a choice
Suffering or with grace

Realistically though, sadness will arise
Afterall, we are human
Sometimes I feel sad too
Though I'm learning to flow

To release all attachment
Allow emotions to wax and wane

Without judgment or force
There is no right way

In this journey, we don't need to go alone
With the support of community we grow
No need to isolate
I am whole

I wish to be seen as a warrior
With peace and grace
Able to master and harness the energy
In my own way

9 – Yoni

Life is an orgasm
In human form

Only created in a sacred portal
Channeled through the womb

An incredibly adaptable force
Able to transmute dimension and depths
A vortex of flow and water
That cannot be contained in mere words

The yoni is divine
A portal to source

Granted the utmost power
An ability to create life

Yin and Yang
Delicate and fierce
Powerful enough to push through birth
Yet soft and nurturing to develop life

In full bloom
A lotus

Soft

Open

Surrendered

In full force

A warrior

Strong

Determined

Withstanding

In rawest form

A wild woman

Liberated

Enticing

Wet

Resilient beyond comprehension

Shedding and rebuilding

Every month

Self-healing and repairing

After birth

Where a seed gets planted

Gentle pulsations of life

An incredibly powerful force
Able to transcend space and time
Void where something gets created from nothing
A miracle that cannot be contained in words

Though easily dominated
Sometimes overridden
By masculine forces

It feels every stroke and sensation
Tolerable, pleasurable and everything in between
Listen to what it needs

Remember the feminine is divine
Honor its boundlessness

Yoni
Courier of life

Creator in human form
And what makes life continue on

10 – Snake

I am a snake
That kundalini rising

I shed time and time again
Leaving behind old skeletons

Peel apart my layers
My core still remains

Can't keep me caged
I'll slither away

Depths they can't see
Brews underneath

Stillness in silence
Plotting my next move

Gaze into my eyes
You don't know what I am capable of

I crush predators
Through sheer flexibility

Wrapping them around my finger
Unaware of what's happening

A fluid spine
Your strongest ally

Adaptability in different environments
My venom

Curled on a pole
Or exploring the earth

Weaving through the jungle and mountains
The world is my playground

Climbing at different heights
I see from many angles

I pierce through challenges like venom
A subtle slow and steady burn

Throw me around, I won't get swayed
See me rise from the center

I am a snake
That kundalini rising

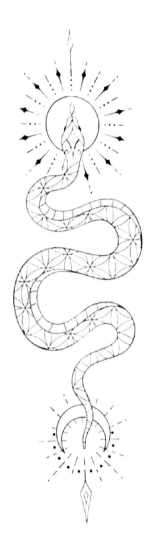

Part 3

Ego says:

once everything falls into place, I'll feel peace.

Spirit says:

find your peace and then everything will fall into place.

Anonymous Instagram post

11 – Ping

In a world with so many tunes
It's easy to get muddled
Mimicking others for acceptance

So I come to a place of silence
To find my own rhythm
Get in touch with my inner world

Clearing out the noise
Emotions arise, violent explosions at first
They have been suppressed

Get a grip on yourself
Learn the ways of ancient wisdom
Tame the wild unrefined wild energy

Slowly normalizing over time
Swings become less volatile
Coming and going like gentle waves

Continue to harness the energy
With precision and practice, like sharpening a knife
Cut straight through the noise

Dissonance distilled and purified
A regulated self
Transmuted clean energy

One clear, crisp note at a time
Somehow flows into a melody
Ready to be shared

Learning to vibrate at my own frequency
In my own song
I can finally hear my voice

Finally, clairvoyance
Clarity in the silence
Still presence to be felt

Wisdom begins to channel easily
Like downloads from the cosmos
Deep knowing within

Fewer words to be said
Presence to be felt
Silence to be admired

Ping

An angelic, pure sound
New vibration and energy
Nothing can change its frequency

12 – Welcome home

The day I left for India
I stepped foot on a new journey
To come home to myself
Deeper than I ever have before

Time away to
Clear my mind
Mend my heart
Heal my body

Learn to be with myself
To feel like myself
My life on pause
Be in the void (oh the suspense!)

No attachments back home
Work to rediscover who you are
Turn completely inwards
Stillness

A yearning for healing
A need to evolve higher
A desire for love
Many clear, planted intentions

To come home stronger and grounded

Braver and wiser than ever
Heal, so you don't repeat old patterns
Ready to live and love like never before

After being away for 4 months
So many loose ends to sort
Sell the house, where to live, find more work
One step at a time

I return home proud of the shifts it took
Of no longer running away
Braver to face and embrace it
Stillness in the midst of uncertainty

Grounded in the cyclone of chaos
Open ended items swirling around
I hold my center
Peace at the core

Not gonna lie
It's overwhelming
Though with new tools and skills
I feel more at ease

Day in and day out
Stick with your practice
Integrate learnings from India
Wherever I am in the world

Welcome home, they'll say
Little will they see
There has always been a sense of home
Within me

Excited to welcome a new life
Adventure awaits
For the life and love I seek
Is all within reach

13 – Hi Michelle

Hi Michelle

It's good to see you again
It's been a while
Your smile has returned
It's nice to hear you laugh

Where'd you go?
Well that sounds far
I'm glad it was good
Because you haven't been yourself for sometime now

Ah, so that's what happened
I had no idea
Makes sense now
You were so distant and small

Sorry you went through that
Sounds like it's been rough
Relieved and happy to hear you're through the other side
How'd you do it?

It's cool you're speaking again
You've been so quiet
You have a good voice
I like when you share

For a while I was worried

At least now you have all these lessons learned
It's nice to have time to yourself
You had to feel it to heal it
Experience it deeply and work through it
To let it go

Healing work sounds hard
I can only imagine
Though I can feel your shift
There's something different

Haha
I forgot how weird you were
Your weirdness is funny though
Just keep being you

So what's next?
That's okay to not know
Go with the flow
I'm excited to see where your journey goes

2023, what a helluva year
Everything will be okay
Don't overthink
You'll know when you know
You're just planting seeds for 2024

At least with what you've been through
You'll never forget
And now you have a book of poems
For you to look back

Remember this time
With beauty and grace
You'll never be in this stage ever again
So look back at it with gratitude

I have no doubt, you'll do great things
One step at a time
It always comes together
Make sure to treat yourself kind

Last but not least
Incase you forget
I love you
I am proud of you
I'll leave it at that

About Michelle Yu

Michelle is a second-generation Chinese American born and raised in the suburbs of Los Angeles. As the daughter of immigrants and refugees, she found this added complexity to her identity and worldview. Since childhood, Michelle turned to writing and journaling as a place of solace to process her convoluted thoughts.

Michelle is a coach, consultant and speaker who is passionate about health, wellbeing and raising consciousness. She holds a Bachelor's degree from UC Irvine and MBA from Duke University Fuqua School of Business. She enjoys yoga, traveling, and being in nature. When she's not out exploring the world, she resides (mostly) in Los Angeles.

www.michellekyu.com